Fresh & Fun

Teaching With
Kids' Names

BY BOB KRECH

PROFESSIONAL BOOKS

NEW YORK • TORONTO • LONDON • AUCKLAND • SYDNEY
MEXICO CITY • NEW DELHI • HONG KONG

To Mom and Dad

ACKNOWLEDGMENTS

Thanks to the many great teachers who helped with ideas, photos, and samples for this book:
Bethany Cantrell, Marianne Chang, Jackie Clarke, Patricia Conover, Denise Dauler, Tina Dickinson,
Rick Ellis, Abbie Ford, Kristen Gephart, Elaine Magud, Judy Meagher, Carole Moore,
Charlotte Sassman, Judi Shilling, Susan Thomas, and Russ Walsh.
Thanks also to my 1998–1999 second grade students at Dutch Neck School for their help
in trying out many of the activities in this book.

CREDITS

"How to Tell a Camel" from *A Hippopotamusn't and Other Animal Poems by J. Patrick Lewis.*
Copyright © 1990 by J. Patrick Lewis. Reprinted by permission of Dial Books for Young Readers,
a division of Penguin Putnam USA Inc.

"Yellow" by David McCord from *AWAY AND AGO: RHYMES OF THE NEVER WAS AND ALWAYS IS*
by David McCord. Copyright © 1968, 1974 by David McCord. Reprinted by permission of Little, Brown
and Company.

Edited by Joan Novelli
Front cover, interior, and poster design by Kathy Massaro
Cover and interior art by Shelley Dieterichs, except page 26 by James Graham Hale
Poster art by Laura Merer

ISBN 0-439-06267-5

Contents

About This Book

The old adage asks, "What's in a name?" Where children are concerned the obvious answer is, "Everything!" Few things capture children's attention more quickly than seeing and hearing their own names. Their names are among the first words children learn to read and write. This, along with the natural excitement and interest children have about names, particularly their own, makes *Names* a perfect theme for connecting skills and concepts across the curriculum.

Names is a great theme for any time of the year. Students begin each and every year learning the names of new classmates, friends, and teachers. As the year progresses, *Names* remains an interest in every area of the curriculum—names of characters in books, animals in science, places in social studies, songs in music, as well as the new kid in class and the new bus driver. Any time a child finds his or her own name in a story, game, song, or activity there is an instant surge in focus, motivation, and enjoyment.

What's equally interesting about names is that, in addition to our own names and our friends' names, there are names everywhere around us—stores, restaurants, cereals, states, countries, even planets! Many of these activities build on that connection and bring students' viewpoints from the simple beginning of "my name" out to the rest of the world around them while stretching their conception of what names are about.

You'll find this book filled with a wide variety of activities from teachers around the country—from quick and instant time-fillers for those spur-of-the-moment activities to projects with plenty of opportunity for kids to dig in deep. As you review the lessons you will find all the senses and modes of expression are engaged and stretched. Kids will sing, paint, clap, draw, play, create, think, research, and smile as they get into *Names*. Some of the kinds of activities inside include:

- fun reading and writing skill-builders
- name games
- literature-based language arts activities
- interactive bulletin boards
- hands-on math and science activities
- easy and appealing art projects
- ideas that combine movement with learning
- learning center suggestions
- reproducible templates
- "The Amazing Name Game"— big, colorful poster

The fifty-plus activities here are organized by content areas. As you would expect in early elementary curriculum, most of the ideas naturally integrate a number of disciplines. You can use this book to create an in-depth unit of study on names by selecting an activity or two from each content area to build a multi-disciplinary approach appropriate to your class and level. Or you may want to guide your class through an exploration of names with one particular discipline like math or language arts. The activities will also come in handy if you're looking for that one special project or instant lesson. It's up to you. Children are always interested in names.

Teaching With the Poster: The Amazing Name Game

This board game invites children to build names using letter squares, developing spelling skills along the way. Students might spell their names, names of states or other places, names of animals or flowers, names for objects, and so on. There are many possibilities. Use the names on the game board for more ideas. Follow these steps to set up and play the game.

◎ Make five copies of page 32. Laminate, then cut apart the letter squares.

◎ Laminate the poster (bound in back of book) for durability.

◎ Place the letter squares face down next to the game board.

◎ Each player selects a bank of ten letter squares to begin.

◎ The first player rolls a die, moves the number of spaces indicated, and follows any directions in that space. This player tries to spell a name with his or her letter squares and places the name to the side. Players may opt to allow one name per turn, or more. Play continues with each player rolling the die, moving, and trying to spell a name.

◎ The game is over when the first player reaches the end of the game board. Students can count up the names they've spelled to see who wins. For a collaborative version, have students work together to make names.

TIP

This game is best played by groups of 2 to 4 children. Children may have fun making their own versions of The Amazing Name Game. They can design games on posterboard using the poster as a model.

Teacher Share

Give Me an A!

Write each student's name on a sentence strip and place them all in a bag. Each day pull one of the sentence strips out and display it on the board. Invite students to do a letter cheer of the name chosen: "Give me an A! Give me an M! Give me a Y! What does it spell? AMY!" Finish with a big round of applause. As students become proficient, let them take over picking out the name and leading the cheer.

Tina Dickinson
Lindbergh Elementary School
Little Falls, Minnesota

Teacher Share

What's in a Name?

To help familiarize children with their names, and the individual letters of their names, try this activity.

◎ Write the letters of each child's first and last name on "letter cards," one letter per card. (You can use unlined index cards cut in half. Use two colors—one for vowels, one for consonants. Or, copy the letter reproducibles on page 32 on different colors of paper.) Place each child's letter cards in a separate envelope and write the child's name on it.

◎ Give students the envelopes with their name cards and let them work with the letter cards, putting them together to spell their names and any other words they can. Have students record the words they spell and store these lists in their envelopes.

◎ Once students have played with the letter cards for their own names, have them exchange cards with classmates and do the same.

◎ Store envelopes in a labeled box to create a portable learning station.

Marianne Chang
Schilling School
Newark, California

Who Stole the Cookies From the Cookie Jar?

This familiar verse (right) is repeated with great zest and bounce by young children. Turn it into an engaging pocket-chart activity by writing each line on a sentence strip. Write students' names on sentence strips and trim to fit. Place the names in a cookie jar (or decorated coffee can or large yogurt container). Have a student choose a name from the jar and place it in the blank space on the pocket chart. Chant the verse together. Let the student whose name was chosen be the next one to pick a name from the cookie jar. Continue until the jar is empty.

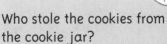
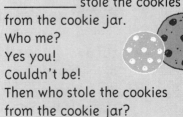

Who stole the cookies from the cookie jar?
_____ stole the cookies from the cookie jar.
Who me?
Yes you!
Couldn't be!
Then who stole the cookies from the cookie jar?

A My Name is Alice

by Jane Bayer (Dial Books, 1984)

Discuss the pattern that is repeated throughout this familiar jump rope rhyme.

____ my name is _____ and my friend's name is _____.
We come from _____ and we sell _____.

Use the reproducible mini-book on page 13 to let students rewrite the rhyme with their names. Have children complete the blanks on each page and illustrate, then cut apart the pages and staple them in order to make the book. (They may want to make and add cover pages first.) Invite children to read aloud their books to the class or a small group. If possible, take the activity outside or to the gym, where students can put their jump rope rhymes into action!

TIP

As a variation, you can have children copy and complete the rhyme on large sheets of paper. Bind pages together to create a class Big Book.

Teacher Share

Is Your Name the Same?

Have each child print his or her name in big letters at the top of a sheet of paper. About two-thirds of the way down the paper, have children draw a horizontal line. Now let children visit with one another to discover if their names have letters in common. Have children write their names in blue above the line if they have letters in common with the child whose name is at the top of the paper. Have them circle the letters they have in common. If they have no letters in common, have children write their names in green below the line.

Denise Dauler
El Carmelo School
Palo Alto, California

Book Break

Chrysanthemum
by Kevin Henkes (Greenwillow, 1991)

After showing students the cover of the book and reading the title, ask: *Does anyone know what a chrysanthemum is?* Allow time for ideas, then share the story. Follow up by discussing the main character's name. Ask: *Why do you think Chrysanthemum's parents named her that? Does anyone know other people or characters who are named after flowers or other things?* (such as *Violet, Rose, Ruby, Pearl*) Bring in a couple of baby name books and help students find the origins of their names. Students might like to make name plates to hang on their desks, complete with illustrations that represent what their names mean.

First Letter Name Poems

Here's an easy list poem based on the first letter of children's names. Have each child write his or her name at the top of a sheet of paper. To write their poems, have children list words that describe them, or something they like or are good at, that also start with the first letter of their name. For example, Masami might write:

Masami

Musical
Mountain climber
Michael's friend
Magic
Movies
Monopoly
Marshmallows

Book Break

D.W. All Wet
by Marc Brown (Little, Brown, 1988)

Marc Brown's Arthur is a very popular character with children, as is his little sister, D.W. Read *D.W. All Wet*, or one of the other books about Arthur's sister, to your students. Explain that the letters *D.W.* are the initials of her name. Ask children what the initials might stand for. Record guesses on a chart, reminding students who know the answer not to give it away.

Have students write their first and last names on paper. You may want to write younger students' names for them. Ask students to circle the first letter of their first name and the first letter of their last name to determine their initials. Let students make name tags using their initials. Punch a hole at the top of each tag and string with yarn. Let children wear their initial name tags for the day. Wrap up the activity by sharing *Arthur Gets the Chicken Pox* (Little, Brown, 1994), where it is revealed that D.W. stands for Dora Winifred.

Computer Connection

Build vocabulary in English and Spanish with *Usborne's Animated First Thousand Words* (Usborne; Win/Mac CD-ROM). As they visit each of thirty-five everyday scenes, children will hear words read aloud, record words, match words and pictures, sort, and more.

Teacher Share

Who Am I?

Memory games are fun to do with most every subject area. It is even more fun for students if they themselves are the subjects! Take a photograph of each student in the class. Glue each photo to a large index card. On another set of index cards write students' names in large, bold letters. Shuffle the cards and place them face down in the middle of a circle of players. To play, have students take turns flipping over two cards. If the picture and name match, the student keeps the set. If not, the cards get turned over. Students can play until they match all of the cards.

Tina Dickinson
Lindbergh Elementary School
Little Falls, Minnesota

TIP

You can also set up students' photo and name cards at a table and let children visit in pairs or alone to match cards.

Letter Scavenger Hunt

Children always enjoy a scavenger hunt. To begin this hunt give each student a sheet of lined paper. Have students write their names at the top in large letters. (Encourage them to leave a little space between each letter.) Have students create columns by drawing lines that extend the length of the paper between each letter. Tell students they are about to go on a Letter Scavenger Hunt. Ask them to hunt around the room for words beginning with the letter in each column. Decide together where students can look for words— for example, words that name objects, words that are part of displays, words in books, names of people in the room, and so on. The goal is to have at least one word in each column. You can vary this by having students go for two, three, or any number of words in a letter column.

You're in the Story!

All children like to hear stories about themselves, or read stories with characters who have the same name. Have students work with you to write a simple story, taking turns supplying characters, a setting, a beginning, a simple problem, a solution, and an ending. Write the story on chart paper. Each time you come to a character's name, draw a rather long line to create a blank.

When the story is finished, have students write their names on individual sentence strips. Trim and laminate. Return to the story chart and begin to read the story aloud with the class, this time inserting a name card wherever the character's name would go. (You can use removable wall adhesive to hold the sentence strips in place.) Have the class read this version of the story. The more exciting, descriptive, or silly the story is, the more fun students have when you insert a name. Repeat to make sure everyone has a chance to be in the story.

Teacher Share

Class Names Bingo Board

Play "Name Bingo," good for reinforcing letter recognition. Make copies of the Bingo board on page 12. Have students fill them in by writing their names and/or the names of classmates, one letter in each box. Students can use first names, last names, or both. (Names can run over from one line to the next. Post a class list of names if students need help spelling them.) The center space is "free." While students are making Bingo boards, make a copy of page 32 and cut apart the letter squares. Give students game markers (dried beans work well) and you're ready to play. Select a letter square at random. Call out the letter and have children place a marker over that letter in as many places as it appears on their cards. When students have filled in letters to make a name, have them call it out.

Bethany Cantrell
Schilling School
Newark, California

Teacher Share

Name Puzzles

Sandhya

These easy-to-make puzzles let students learn about letters, sounds, spelling, and names—their own and their classmates'. Print each student's name on a sentence strip and laminate. Cut each name apart to make puzzle pieces. (For the simplest puzzle, keep letters intact.) Put each name puzzle in an envelope. Write the student's name on the outside. Keep the envelopes together in a box labeled "Name Puzzles." Let students pick individual envelopes from the box and put the name puzzles together. Provide a copy of a class list in the box so children can check off the puzzles they've completed. Challenge students to see how many names they can put together.

Bethany Cantrell
Schilling School
Newark, California

Write Me a Letter

Encourage the art of letter-writing (and learning names) with this activity. Provide blank paper and letter stamps. Have children use the letter stamps to write their names at the top of the paper. They can draw small pictures or designs next to their names. Make copies of each child's paper. Children can use their stationery to write letters to friends and family members.

COmPUter Connection

Children will also enjoy using *Kid Pix Deluxe* (Broderbund) to make personalized stationery. They can use the alphabet stamps or type tool to write their names, and rubber stamps to add favorite pictures.

Names Around the World

Talk with students about the idea that words are names for things. For example, their names are words for themselves. Point out that there are many languages around the world and so many ways to say the same thing. If there are children in your class who are multilingual, let them tell names for things in the classroom in their native languages. Bring in a few foreign language dictionaries to learn more. How many ways can they find to say the same thing? Words like *hello* or *thank-you* are very good starter words, as are simple nouns like *head* or *nose*.

Name _____ Date _____

Class Names Bingo Board

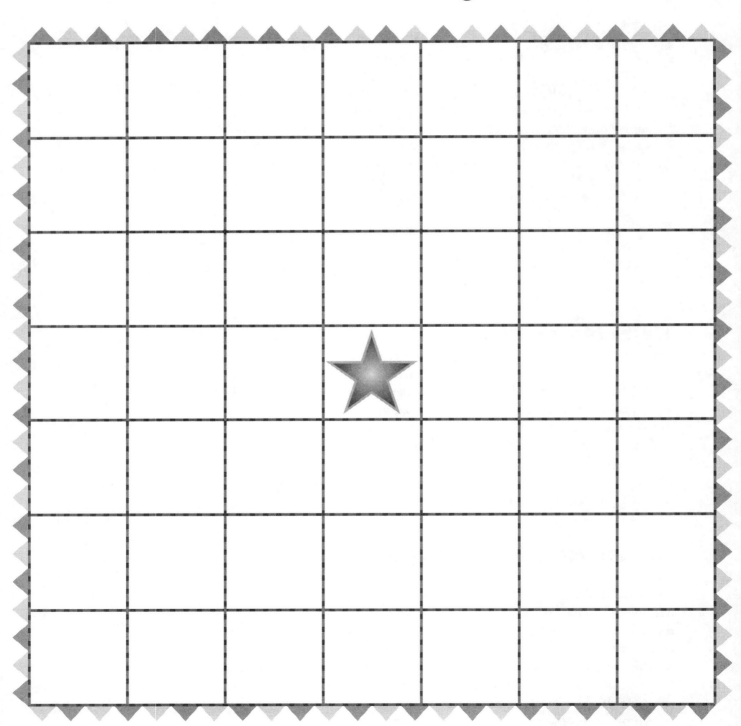

My name is

....

1

and my friend's name is

....

2

We come from

....

3

and we sell

....

4

Teacher Share

Class Names Number Sort

Children can begin to learn common mathematical comparison vocabulary using their own names to provide the number data. Use a couple of sheets of large squared graph paper (1-by-1-inch is good). Write each child's name on the graph paper—one letter to a square, one name on a line—until you have a complete class list. Make a copy for each student. Have students cut out each name so they have a complete set.

Give each student a large (11-by-17-inch) "sorting paper" which is divided in thirds with the three sections labeled "Fewer Letters Than My Name," "Same Number of Letters as My Name," and "More Letters Than My Name." Have students begin by gluing their own names in the middle section. Now have children sort the rest of their classmates' names into one of the three categories by counting how many letters are in each and then gluing the name down in the appropriate section. When children are finished sorting, invite them to make comparisons: *How many students have names with more letters than their own? Fewer? The same as? What other comparisons can children make?*

Judi Shilling
Dutch Neck School
Princeton Junction, New Jersey

TIP

Use the book *Chrysanthemum* for more math fun. (See Book Break, page 8.) Ask students to quickly guess how many letters are in this character's name. Then ask if they think there's anyone in the school with more letters in his or her first name. Find out!

How Many Letters?

How many letters do most children have in their names? Give each child a copy of the graph on page 17. Have students count the number of letters in their names, then fill in a box above that number. For example, John would fill in a square above the number 4. So would Sara. Corina would fill in a square above the 6. Let students fill in a square on each classmate's graph to show how many letters in their names. (Each student will then have a class graph.) Discuss what the graph shows. You can build the same graph with Unifix cubes for a physical representation. For a more in-depth project, students can survey other classes and gather and graph this larger set of data. Try the graphs with last names and number of syllables, too.

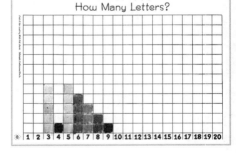

Activity Page
How Many Letters?

1 2 3 4 5 6 7 8 9 10 11 12 13 14 15 16 17 18 19 20

Names Add Up

You'll need a pile of pennies and nickels for this activity. Explain to children that for this activity, vowels in their names will be worth a nickel and consonants will be worth a penny. Have children take the coins that correspond to the letters in their first names and add them up to find the value of their names—for example, Tim: 1 + 5 + 1 = 7¢. (See sample.) What comparisons can they make? Follow up by challenging children with these questions.

◎ What is the most valuable five-letter name you can think of? The most valuable three-letter name?

◎ What word do you think will be the most valuable?

◎ What would happen to the values if consonants were worth a nickel and vowels a penny?

Have children show calculations to back up their answers.

Name ___Ashley___

Consonants are worth 1¢.

Vowels are worth 5¢.

How much is the name Tim worth? Show your work.
_____Tim_____
1¢ 5¢ 1¢

How much is your name worth? ___18¢___
_____Ashley_____
5¢ 1¢ 1¢1¢ 5¢ 5¢

How much is your teacher's name worth? ___11¢___
___Mr. krech___
1¢ 1¢ 1¢ 1¢ 5¢ 1¢ 1¢

Secret Name Code

Kids love secret codes. Many real codes have number and letter associations of various types. For an easy code, match every letter with its ordinal position in the alphabet—for example, A = 1, B = 2, Z = 26. Get children started on the code, then have them make their own Code-Cracking Decoder Charts. Once everyone has a chart, have students use the code to create math problems that will yield answers that correspond to each letter of their name. (See sample.)

Once students have created their problems, gather their papers and hand them out at random to the class. Have students solve the equations to find out whose code they cracked, then return the papers to their owners. For more secret-code fun, see Book Break, below.

A	B	C	D	E	F	G	H	I	J	K	L	M	N	O	P	Q	R	S	T	U
1	2	3	4	5	6	7	8	9	10	11	12	13	14	15	16	17	18	19	20	21

V	W	X	Y	Z
22	23	24	25	26

A SHORT NAME	SOMEONE YOU KNOW!	YOUR NAME
5 + 5 = J	10 + 3 = M	20 + 1 =
100 − 99 = A	9 + 9 = R	21 − 2 =
7 + 7 = N		1 + 7 =
9 − 4 = E	10 + 1 = K	3 − 2 =
	19 − 1 = R	21 − 2 =
	0 + 5 = E	2 − 1 =
	2 + 1 = C	2 + 1 =
	4 + 4 = h	12 + 2 =
		3 + 1 =
		8 − 1 =
		2 − 1 =

···· **Book Break** ····

How to Keep a Secret: Writing and Talking in Code

by Elizabeth James (Lothrop, Lee & Shepard, 1998)

Through an encoded mystery, readers learn how to create and decipher codes.

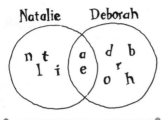

An Alphabet Chart

Ask your students to guess (quickly) how many *As* appear in their names all together. *Bs*? *Cs*? Continue, letting children make guesses for each letter of the alphabet. To check guesses, make a giant alphabet chart. Write each letter of the alphabet on an index card. Tape these up across a large space. Have each child write his or her name on index cards, one letter per card. One at a time, have them tape up their cards under the appropriate letters on the chart. Which letter appears most often in students' names? Least? Extend the study to chart letters in names of students in your grade or the whole school. Are students' results consistent with their original findings?

Symmetrical Names

Children find the idea of mirror images and symmetry almost magical, and always fun to explore. Give children tracing paper or lightweight drawing paper and have them fold their papers in half. Using a pencil, have children write their names down one side of the paper on the fold. Have children turn the paper over and trace their names on the other side in mirror image. Children can color in their mirror-image names with markers or crayons. A variation for more nimble fingers is to cut this name shape out, including the negative spaces formed by the inside of the letters. This forms a more intricate, detailed design with most names.

Shapes Have Names

A fun way to help kids learn the names of basic shapes is to give those shapes some character.

Make templates for patterns you want to teach. Have students trace the shapes on white drawing paper. Do the same on the board or easel. Explain to students that you would like them to add some "character" to their shapes to help them come alive. Draw a square as an example. Say, "*Square* starts with an *S*, so I'm going to name my square with a first name that starts with an *S*. What could I name it?" List names, such as *Sammy, Sarina, Steve, Sonja,* and so on.

Sonja

square

Choose a name for your square and write it above the picture. Then ask students what kind of drawing details you could add to make the shape seem more like a person. Eyes, mouth, hair, and hat are common responses. Ask students to name their shapes and turn them into Shape People by adding similar details.

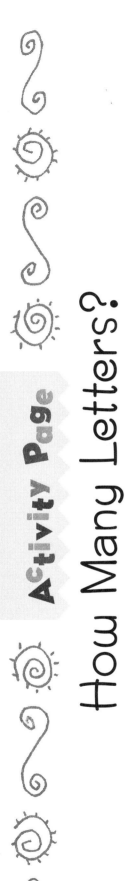

How Many Letters?

1	2	3	4	5	6	7	8	9	10	11	12	13	14	15	16	17	18	19	20

Favorite Food Name Game

To help children get acquainted at the beginning of the year, learn one another's names, and stretch their memory skills, try this activity. Have children sit together in one circle or a number of smaller circles. Begin the activity by saying your name aloud and telling the group your favorite food such as, "My name is Mrs. Davis and my favorite food is spaghetti."

The child next to you in the circle continues the game by reintroducing you to the group saying, "This is Mrs. Davis and she likes spaghetti." This child then introduces herself in the same way: "I'm Gina and I like peaches." The next student continues this cumulative process introducing both Mrs. Davis and Gina and their favorite foods, then introducing himself and his favorite food. ("This is Mrs. Davis, she likes spaghetti. This is Gina, she likes peaches. I'm Pablo and I like pizza.")

As each child tells what his or her favorite food is, ask everyone to try to visualize that student and the food he or she named. This visual cue really aids memory. After going around the circle once, invite volunteers to try to recite the names and foods all the way around the circle.

TIP

Children will enjoy using empty cup-size milk cartons to build houses and other structures to create a 3-D bulletin board community. To make it easy to attach the milk cartons to the bulletin board, cut out the bottoms. Going through the bottom of the cartons, use push pins to display them on the board.

Building Our Community

Tack up a large sheet of green, white, or brown roll paper. Tell students that they will be working together to create a community on this paper "ground." Lead the class in a discussion about the basic needs of a community, such as air, food, water, clothes, and shelter. Spend a few minutes discussing shelter in particular. Talk about the different kinds of places that provide shelter: apartments, mobile homes, condos, houses, and so on. Provide students with materials, then let them work together to create shelters for their community. It can be a shelter that looks like the one they presently live in, or it can be one they would like to live in some day. You may get some castles!

Have students put their names on their houses and glue them to the board. Let students fill out the board with shops, playgrounds, schools, and other parts of their community, giving each place a name. Have students arrange these extras on the board, then work together to name their class community.

Teacher Share

Class Phone Book

Create one of the most popular reference books in any kindergarten or first grade class— a class phone book! Students will enjoy helping to create this highly sought-after book. Make copies of the template on page 21 for each child. Have children complete the information. (You will want to send a note home first, requesting parents' permission to include this information for their children.) Copy a photo of each child (black and white copies are fine) and have them glue these in place on their pages. (They could also draw pictures of themselves.) For individual copies to send home, make a class set of the pages, collate, and bind. Laminate the originals and bind for a class copy.

A picture of you goes here.

Name

Address

Phone

E-mail

Rick Ellis
Dutch Neck School
Princeton Junction, New Jersey

TIP

You can get a lot of mileage out of a basic printed list of class names. Create a list of students' names in alphabetical order (first then last name). Make copies available for students to take and use as they wish. They will think up many uses for this list, such as checking off who is present or absent, who orders what kind of lunch, and so on. Children can also use this list as a spelling reference when they write notes to friends. They also enjoy using the list to gather information for surveys, such as, "Do you have a dog?" or "Do you like the Mets?"

Create a Name

Explain to students that in many cultures throughout history, people have been named according to their abilities, characteristics, or even jobs. For example, long ago a person who made barrels was called a *cooper.* Soon families of barrel makers were known by the last name Cooper.

Some people looked to nature and animals as the sources of their names. Some Native Americans chose or were given names by the older members of their tribe. These names were usually inspired by an attribute, strength, ability, or characteristic of the person. A person who was very fast might have been named Running Deer. One who was very clever might have been called Wise Fox. Focus students' thinking on their abilities and characteristics. Ask: *What name do you think would suit you well? What is special about you? What can you do well?* Have them create names for themselves that use at least two words. Invite them to share the reasons for their new names.

Your Name Is Special

As a take-home activity, invite students to talk with their families about their names. Prepare a simple form that students can bring home that includes questions like: *Why did you name me (child's name)? Are there famous people who share my name?* Students can use their findings to create posters about themselves, titling them with their names. They can add photos, illustrations, and photocopies of documents or special items that help tell about themselves. Give each student an opportunity to share this information and display the poster. This is a wonderful activity for the start of the year.

My Family Tree

Children can begin to learn about the concept of a family tree—and name—with this activity. Introduce the activity by sharing one of the Arthur books by Marc Brown. Guide children in making a simple family tree to show the members of Arthur's family: Arthur, D.W., Mother, Father, Grandma Flora, and so on.

Continue by having children make family trees to show the names of people in their families. On white construction paper, have students paint or draw a tree trunk and branches. Using green paper, have students cut out leaves for their trees, one for each member of the family. On each leaf have students write the name of a family member (including pets if they like). Have children glue the leaves to their "family trees" and write their last names on the trunks. For a fun variation have students make trees and leaves large enough to include a small photograph or a drawing of each family member.

End-of-the-Year Autograph Book

This is a great end-of-the-year activity that provides children with something unique to remember their classmates by. Provide each student with a sheet of paper with space for a picture at the top and lines for writing on the bottom. Have them draw a self-portrait and write a description of themselves, including hints about their identities but not their names. Encourage children not to share their work! Make a class set of each child's paper and collate to make individual autograph books. Give each student a book and have an autograph party! Have students circulate around the room trying to figure out who's who in the book. When they successfully match a classmate to the page, that child autographs his or her page. You can continue this activity over a period of several days to give students plenty of time to collect all signatures.

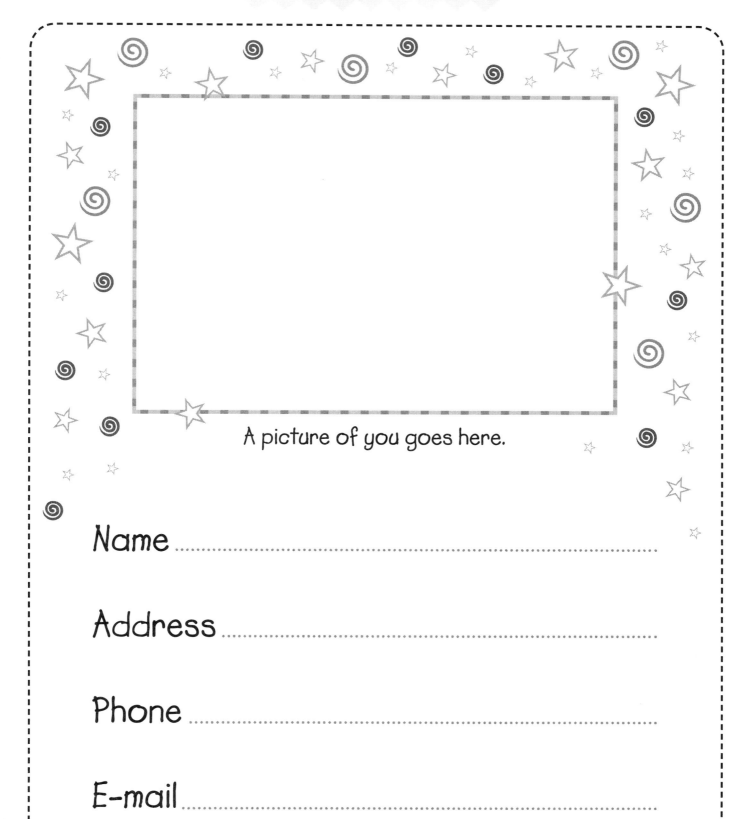

A picture of you goes here.

Name ....

Address ....

Phone ....

E-mail ....

Mystery Writer

Science has always helped investigators solve mysteries. It can help your class solve some, too. Give each child a piece of white drawing paper. Tell children that they will be writing secret messages to the class, then follow these steps.

◎ Have children write a sentence or two in pencil. Ask them to keep their work private and not to put their names on their papers yet.

◎ Provide cups of lemon juice and cotton swabs. Ask children to sign their names with the cotton swab dipped in the lemon juice. Let the notes dry completely.

◎ Read each note aloud. See if children can guess which classmate wrote each note.

◎ Solve the mini-mysteries by applying heat to the "invisible ink." Do this by moving the notes back and forth over a heat source (adult only). In a few seconds the identity of the mystery writer will be revealed. This is most exciting when done with a candle with the lights out. You can also use a light bulb.

◎ Invite children to share explanations for what happened to the "invisible ink" when heat was applied. (*Heat breaks down the carbon compounds in the lemon juice, causing it to turn brown or black. This is the same reaction that causes marshmallows or bread to darken when toasted.*) Discuss other changes caused by heat.

Safety Tip

Caution students not to try this activity at home without adult supervision.

Names in Nature

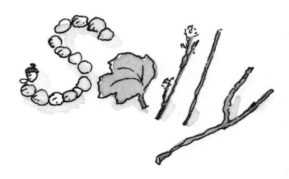

Take your class on a nature walk. Bring along some bags and have students collect twigs, leaves, acorns, pebbles, grass blades, and other small natural objects. Fall is a good time to do this, although every season yields interesting materials. Back in the classroom, invite students to use these found objects to form the letters of their names. They can alter and rearrange, attach, and manipulate any of the objects to help form the letters. After arranging the letters on cardboard mats, have them glue them in place. Students may want to paint the cardboard first. A white background will help the letters stand out. Students can frame their names by gluing leftover materials around the edges of the cardboard.

Teacher Share

Sidewalk Spelling

Gather various sizes of paintbrushes along with plastic containers and go outside to paint names. Pour water into the containers and give each child a paintbrush. Have children use the sidewalk for a canvas. The movements are big and easy for children to master, mistakes are easily erased, and cleanup is a cinch. Ask children to notice what happens to their names. *(They disappear over time.)* Ask: *Why do you think this happens?* Guide children in making a connection between the water on the sidewalk and puddles. *(Both disappear over time, or evaporate.)*

Charlotte Sassman
Alice Carlson Applied Learning Center
Fort Worth, Texas

TIP

Young children may not be able to fully understand the concept of *evaporation*—the process by which water (a liquid) turns into water vapor (a gas), but they can begin to develop an understanding of the water cycle as they paint with water on the sidewalk and see it disappear, or evaporate.

Spell It in Sparkles

Explore the world of crystals with an activity that lets children spell their name in sparkles! Begin by sharing a book about crystals. (See Book Break, below.) Ask children to describe the crystals they see in the pictures. Guide them to recognize a crystal's symmetrical shape. Mix up an Epsom salts solution to spell names in sparkly letters.

◎ Heat 3 cups water until hot but not boiling. Stir in 4 cups Epsom salts, one spoonful at a time. Pour the solution into a glass baking pan. Let cool.

◎ Have children write their names in big block letters and cut them out.

◎ Let children dip their letters in the Epsom salts solution and place them on paper towels to dry. Children can glue their sparkly letters to tag board to make name plates, or tie string to each letter and dangle mobile-style from a coat hanger or stick.

Book Break

Snowflakes, Sugar, and Salt: Crystals Up Close

by Chu Maki (Lerner, 1993)

Children can examine characteristics of everyday crystals with color photographs and simple text. Easy experiments invite further investigation.

Collaborative Color Poems

Explore names for colors with poetry. Start by sharing the poem "Yellow" by David McCord. (See page 26.) Follow up by inviting children to brainstorm things that are yellow. Write their ideas on chart paper to make a list poem. (Start the poem with "Yellow is….") Go further by creating a display of things that are different shades of yellow. Give the different shades of yellow their own names, such as *lemon yellow*, *buttercup*, and *sunflower*.

Invite children to collaborate on a poem about another color. Post chart paper at a display, along with markers and crayons. Write "[color name] is _____" at the top and let children take turns adding lines to build the poem. Again, discuss names for the various shades of the color. Add pictures to the display that represent different shades. Post fresh chart paper for new color poems. Display them around the room or bind to make a Big Book of Color Poetry.

Book Break

Naming Colors
by Adrienne Dewey (HarperCollins, 1995)

Students will be intrigued by information on how colors got their names. They'll also find answers to some curious questions—for example, "What do worms have to do with the color *crimson*?"

Camels Have Names

Tell the class that you are going to share some scientific information with them that not many adults know. Point out to students that there are two kinds of camels in the world and each one has a special name. There is the camel with one hump, which is called a *dromedary*. There is also a second type of camel with two humps, known as the *bactrian* camel. These are their scientific names—they are not so easy to remember, but here is a great poem to help out!

Follow up by letting students cut out the letters *B* and *D* from sturdy paper or posterboard. Have students roll their letters over as you reread the poem aloud.

How to Tell a Camel
The Dromedary has one hump
The Bactrian has two.
It's easy to forget this rule
So here is what to do.
Roll the first initial over
on its flat behind.
The Bactrian is different from
the Dromedary kind.

J. Patrick Lewis

Starry, Starry Names

What names do students know for the stars they see in the sky? The *Big Dipper* and *Little Dipper* might be familiar names. Ask students how they think these groups of stars got their names. Guide them to recognize that the shapes of these groups of stars match their names. Use a book about constellations to learn more about the names people give groups of stars. (See Book Break, below.)

Follow up by letting children create and name their own constellations. Give each child a handful of rock salt and a sheet of black or dark blue paper. Have them drop pieces of rock salt on the paper, glue them in place, and draw a line around the shape. Let students decide what their groups of stars look like and give their constellations names.

Book Break

Glow-in-the-Dark Night Sky Book
by Clint Hatchett (Random House, 1988)

Pull the shades, switch off the lights, and watch the constellations pictured in this book light up.

Hurricane Who?

Arlene, Bret, Cindy, Dennis, Emily…these aren't names on a class list. They're names on the National Hurricane Center's list. Ask students if they know why hurricanes have names. Let them try to find their names on a list of hurricanes, including the International Name List. (See Computer Connection.) Look for news about hurricanes in the newspaper or on the Internet. To go further, launch an investigation on wind with these connections.

◎ Make wind socks and wind vanes to study the wind's strength and direction. Simple directions are available in *A Year of Hands-On Science* by Lynne Kepler (Scholastic Professional Books, 1996).

◎ Find and share weather lore about the wind—for example, *A wind from the west brings weather at its best. A wind from the east brings rain to man and beast.* Ask children to discuss ways they can find out if good or bad weather is coming their way.

Computer Connection

Learn more about hurricane names by visiting the National Hurricane Center web site at **www.nhc.noaa. gov/** Click on "The Naming of Storms." You can also find a glossary of hurricane vocabulary here, as well as satellite imagery of storms.

Yellow

Green is go,
and red is stop
and yellow is peaches
with cream on top.

Earth is brown,
and blue is sky;
yellow looks well
on a butterfly.

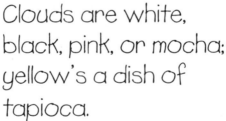

Clouds are white,
black, pink, or mocha;
yellow's a dish of
tapioca.

—David McCord

Try This!

◎ Find two words in the poem that rhyme with <u>hop</u>.

◎ Name three things that are yellow.

_____

_____

_____

_____

_____

On the back of this paper, draw a picture of your favorite yellow thing.

Teacher Share

Yell and Spell

Children love to use those big orange traffic cones as megaphones. Well, here's their chance. Divide the class into two groups at one end of the gym or another large space. At the other end place two traffic cones, one opposite each team. Have each group line up single file facing the cones. When a signal is given, the first student in line runs down to the traffic cone, picks it up, and yells/spells out his or her name through it. After each letter is called out, the rest of their team must repeat that letter together as loudly as they can. This continues until the whole name is spelled out and repeated. They then put the cone down, run back, tag the next player, and continue in this way until everyone has had a turn to get in a good run and yell.

Abbie Ford
Dutch Neck School
Princeton Junction, New Jersey

Sculpt and Spell

Here's an easy but interesting way for students to "sculpt" their names. Give each student a two-foot length of string or yarn and a base of wood, paneling, or cardboard. Place dishes of white glue (clean meat trays make good glue-holders) in central locations. Guide students in following these directions to make string sculptures of their names.

◎ Cut the string into pieces to form the letters of your name.

◎ Dip each piece of string in white glue and place on the base in the shape of the letter.

◎ Let the string dry in place.

◎ Paint the base and/or the string if you wish. Contrasting colors work well.

TIP

Students can also use seeds and other materials to sculpt their names.
(See Names in Nature, page 22.)

Teacher Share

Crayon Resist Names

This simple but effective art technique is made even better when a child's name is the focus. Provide each student with a piece of heavy white construction paper or drawing paper. Ask children to write their names on the paper with crayon, going over it three or four times to make sure the crayon is layered on thickly. Encourage the use of a variety of colors such as reds, yellows, and oranges. Have students use watercolors to paint over their names with a darker color like blue or purple. The crayon will resist the paint, but the rest of the paper will pick it up. Students' names will stand out bright and bold!

Elaine Magud
Joshua Cowell School
Manteca, California

Book Break

"The Yipiyuk" from Where The Sidewalk Ends

by Shel Silverstein (HarperCollins, 1974)

The poetry of Shel Silverstein never fails to delight children, especially when he is describing a creature with a very strange and interesting name like *Yipiyuk*. What's a Yipiyuk? Read aloud Shel Silverstein's poem, "The Yipiyuk" from *Where the Sidewalk Ends*. Be sure not to show children the illustration in the book. When you have finished the poem, ask everyone to draw a picture of what they think the Yipiyuk looks like based on what they heard in the poem. Give everyone a copy of the poem to re-read as they work. Display the Yipiyuks. As a follow-up ask students to create their own strange creatures, name them, and even write a poem about them.

Hidden Animals

Children's names really come alive with this activity. Have students write their names quite large on sheets of white drawing paper. Then have them trace the lines in each letter with thick black marker. Ask them to look carefully at the shapes that the letters form. Do any of these shapes suggest an animal or part of an animal or several animals? Invite students to add lines, shapes, and textures to transform the letters of their names into animals—real or imagined! Encourage students to be creative. A whole zoo might be contained in a name!

Book Break

Animals A to Z
by David McPhail (Scholastic, 1989)

Ant, armadillo, bear, bird, cricket, crocodile... there are animals for every letter of the alphabet in this book—even X. What animal names do your students know for each letter of the alphabet? Let them make their own animal alphabet books with animal names of their own—pets included!

Teacher Share

Scoot and Spell

This is a good game for using the sit-down scooters that are very popular in gym classes, but it can also be played just by running or "crab walking." Divide the class into two teams. Have students line up along parallel lines facing each other with a hula hoop in the middle of the floor between the teams. Write each letter of the alphabet on a large index card. Make at least four full sets. Put the letter cards in the hula hoop. To play, call out a name. Each team sends one player at a time on the scooter (or running, hopping, skipping, etc.) into the middle to retrieve one letter needed to spell that name. Students shuttle back and forth to the center, retrieving a new letter each time, until the whole target name is correctly spelled. Be sure to have enough letter cards to spell the names you use.

Abbie Ford
Dutch Neck School
Princeton Junction, New Jersey

Hear the Beat

This simple rhythm activity is a fun way to teach about syllabication—and to let students learn more about their own names. Prepare by giving each child a rhythm instrument. You can use wood blocks, tambourines, and cymbals (ask the music teacher to lend an assortment) or simply hands to clap and pencils to tap. Start by introducing a child— say, Melinda—to the class. Have students repeat her name and clap out the syllables, "Me-lin-da." Repeat the name, this time adding a drum beat to the clapping. Continue to repeat the name, adding an instrument or section of instruments each time. The tempo can begin slowly and then, once all the instruments have been added in, be made faster and faster until you signal students to slow the beat down again (and possibly bring down the volume), finished with simple hand-clapping. Give everyone a chance to hear their name "played" over the course of a few days.

Book Break

Drummer Hoff
by Barbara Emberley (Prentice Hall, 1967)

This Caldecott-award-winning picture book features a cumulative, repetitive rhyme that is fun and simple for students to act out.

In the story, one unusually-named soldier after another appears to help set up the pieces of a cannon. First comes Private Parriage with the carriage, then Corporal Farrell with the barrel, Sergeant Chowder with the powder, and so on. Finally Drummer Hoff "fires it off!" Every name in the story rhymes with a piece of the cannon or a job they do.

After reading aloud the story, let students dramatize it. Assign students parts in the story. Read it aloud again, this time letting students act out each soldier's part. Let everyone chime in on the "Boom!" at the end. Rotate actors so everyone who wants can play a part.

Passing Pattern Game

This is a great ice-breaker for the beginning of the year, and a good way for children to learn one another's names. Make circles of five to ten students in a group. Give a ball to one student. Have this child pass the ball to another child in the circle. Before passing the ball, however, this child must call out the name of the receiver. The receiver passes the ball to a different child, calling out this child's name. Play continues until each child has been the receiver. The group then repeats the passing pattern several times, then starts over, creating a new passing pattern. For a challenge, play with larger and larger groups, challenging children to remember the order in which the ball was passed with increasing numbers of players.

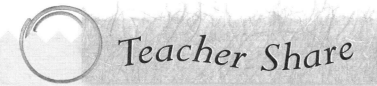

Teacher Share

Sing Those Sounds

Here is a fun and easy song to help students with initial consonant or vowel sounds in their names. Start with students seated on the floor or in their chairs. Begin to sing "Names begin with (insert a letter). Names begin with (letter). Come on up in front, if your name begins with (letter)." Once students with that letter come up, the whole group sings, "Hip Hip Hooray, his/her/their name/s begin/s with (letter)." Repeat this, substituting all the initial letters needed to get everyone up in front. Finally everyone sings, "Hip, hip, hooray, our names begin with…" and then each child shouts out the letter his or her name begins with for a lively ending.

Judy Meagher
Student Teacher Supervisor
Bozeman, Montana

Rainbow Letters

Every word, including every name, has a distinct shape. Have students print their names with black marker on 4-by-12-inch sheets of white paper, then outline the entire shape of their names with a colored marker. Have students choose new marker colors and outline their names again, leaving a little space between the first outline and the second. Have students repeat this pattern, creating a rainbow effect around their names. (You may want to stick more closely to the science of rainbows, exploring rainbows first and having students use the colors in order—red, orange, yellow, green, blue, violet—to outline their names.) These pieces make excellent desktop name labels. Laminate first for durability.

A B C D E

F G H I J

K L M N O

P Q R S T

U V W X Y

Z A E I O